Sorting at the Park

by Cynthia Swain • illustrated by Laurence Knighton

I need to know these words.

gloves

kites

park

sort

Men	Women

Look at the park.
What can you see
at a park?
What can you sort
at a park?

Look at the balloons.
Some balloons are blue.
Some balloons are red.

You can sort the balloons.

Blue	Red

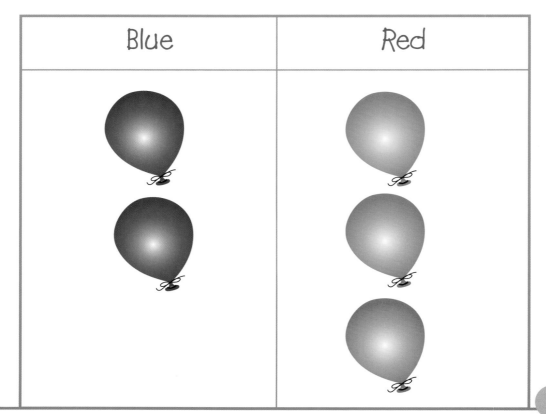

Look at the birds.
Some birds are in
the water. Some birds
are on the grass.

You can sort the birds.

In Water	On Grass

Look at the boys.
Some boys have gloves.
Some boys do not
have gloves.

You can sort the boys.

Boys with Gloves	Boys with No Gloves

Can you see the runners?

Some runners are men.

Some runners are women.

You can sort the runners.

Men	Women

Can you see the kites?
Some kites have tails.
Some kites have no tails.

You can sort the kites.

Tails	No Tails
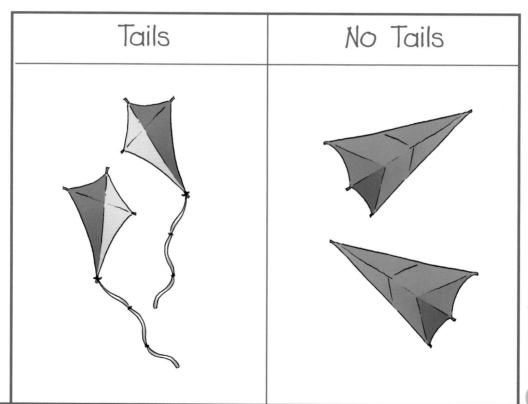	

What can you see
in this park?
What can you sort?